Where Is the Kremlin?

by Deborah Hopkinson

illustrated by Dede Putra

Penguin Workshop

For Dimitri—DH

For Mr. Petrov—DP

PENGUIN WORKSHOP
An Imprint of Penguin Random House LLC, New York

Library of Congress Cataloging-in-Publication Data is available upon request.

ISBN 9781524789749 (paperback)   10 9 8 7 6 5 4 3 2 1
ISBN 9781524789756 (library binding)   10 9 8 7 6 5 4 3 2 1

Contents

Where Is the Kremlin?

Moscow, Russia

One day about seven hundred years ago, two men met in a fort on the top of a hill. Ivan was a prince. Peter was the head of the church in Russia. They gazed out over a deep forest. The year was 1326. The place was the Kremlin.

The word *kremlin* means "fortress" in the Russian language. Up to this time, buildings inside the fort's walls were made of wood. But Prince Ivan wanted buildings that would last. So Ivan and Peter came together to lay the first stone of a new church. They hoped someday their church would stand at the center of a great capital city (Moscow) and a powerful country (Russia).

Their dreams came true. Today, the Dormition Cathedral, the most important church in Russia, sits on this same spot. The seventy acres of the Kremlin are a famous attraction in Moscow, a city of more than twelve million people and the capital of the world's largest country.

The Kremlin is shaped like a triangle. Over time, Moscow has grown up around it in rings. The Kremlin's redbrick walls are more than twelve feet thick. In some places, they rise higher than

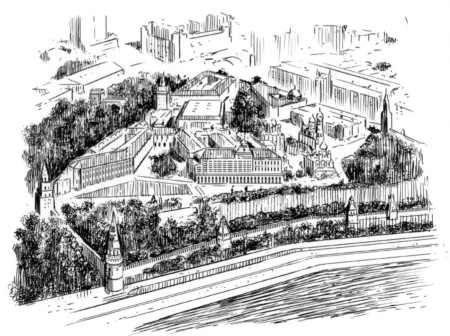

sixty feet. It has twenty towers in all. Nineteen tall ones with spires rise from its walls and seem to touch the sky.

The Kremlin is the official home of the Russian president. It's also the center of government. In a way, the Kremlin is like America's White House, Capitol Building (where Congress meets), National Mall, and the many Smithsonian museums all in one. But the Kremlin is much, much older.

Over its long history, the Kremlin has seen emperors and empresses come and go. Enemy armies have stormed its walls. Fierce fires and invaders have destroyed buildings and artwork.

Visitors today can see jewels, ornate armor, and amazing architecture. But much remains hidden. The Kremlin holds secrets: tales of murder, hidden tunnels, and terrible, cold dungeons.

All this makes the Kremlin one of the most fascinating places in the world.

CHAPTER 1
The Fort on the Hill

The Kremlin and Moscow, the city that grew up around it, lie in the western part of Russia, near Scandinavia and countries around the Baltic Sea. Russia stretches across part of the top of Europe and the top of Asia, all the way to the Pacific Ocean. Russia is larger than China and nearly twice the size of Canada. It spans eleven time zones.

In addition to its great northern forests, Russia boasts mountains, deserts, and flat grasslands called steppes. Russia also contains Arctic tundra. These are places where the ground stays partially frozen all year and no trees grow. Europe's longest river, the Volga, flows through Russia. Lake Baikal, the oldest, deepest, and largest lake in the world, is here, too. The lake contains one-fifth of all the fresh water on earth. It's also home to freshwater seals, the only ones in the world.

Little is known about the people who lived in Russia in ancient times. Many scholars believe that in the early 800s, tribal groups called Slavs settled here. Next came the Vikings, whom most Russian historians call the Rus. Over time, the Rus and the Slavs married one other.

Vikings, known as Rus

Contact with the outside world helped shape Russia's culture, written language, and religion. Around 988, Prince Vladimir of Kiev converted to Eastern Orthodox Christianity, which was the major religion in the Byzantine, or Eastern Roman, Empire. Its capital, Constantinople, is now Istanbul, Turkey. The Russian Orthodox Church became Russia's main religion. People still follow its customs today.

Prince Vladimir of Kiev

Russian Orthodox Church

The Russian Orthodox Church is part of one of three major branches of Christianity. (The other two are Roman Catholic and Protestant.) Like other Christians, followers believe that Jesus was the son of God. But in addition to prayer, fasting and icons are an important part of worship. Icons are paintings of holy figures, such as Jesus. They're used in prayer and often done on a wooden surface.

Even before Prince Ivan's time, there was a fort on the hill in Moscow. It's easy to see why. The spot could be defended easily. Spruce, larch, pine, oak, and fir trees from a nearby forest

European larch plant

provided fuel for warmth and logs for building. Sable (a creature prized for its fur), fox, elk, hare, deer, and beaver supplied food and clothing.

Sable

There was water, too. The Kremlin sits on a bank of the Moscow River. A smaller river once served as a moat.

The first written records that mention Moscow go back to 1147. The first fort dates to 1156. We also have physical evidence that people lived here long ago. Pieces of giant logs have been found, along with the bones of pigs, horses, dogs, and wild game.

Old coins from faraway lands have been found. These tell us that in the tenth century, people in Moscow were trading with other lands. Russian traders sold furs, animal hides, and honey. In return, they bought spices, silk, precious stones, and horses from Asia.

Despite its good defenses, the Kremlin fort couldn't stand up against all attacks. In 1237, Russia was invaded by a ferocious army called the Golden Horde. The invaders came from Mongolia in East Asia. (Today, the nation of Mongolia is

north of China and south of Russia.) The great warrior Genghis Khan founded the Mongol Empire in 1206. Batu, one of his grandsons, led the Russian invasion.

The Golden Horde controlled Russia for more than a century. However, the Mongols didn't meddle much in everyday Russian life. They respected people's religious beliefs and allowed local princes to be in charge of their own areas. But the Mongols did demand tribute payments, just as landlords expect rent.

The Mongols were finally overthrown in 1480
by Ivan III. Sometimes called
Ivan the Great, this ruler also
wanted to make his mark
on the Kremlin fortress.
And indeed he did.

Ivan the Great

Cyrillic Alphabet

The Russian language is written using the Cyrillic alphabet. It was named for Saint Cyril, who invented the writing system in the ninth century.

The Russian alphabet contains thirty-three letters and signs. Some Cyrillic letters look and sound similar to English. For example, *a* is pronounced like the *a* in *father.* Others look the same but sound different. In Russian, *p* sounds like *r* in the word *error.* And some letters don't look anything like ours.

The Orthodox Church also follows a different calendar. It's slightly different from the one used by many Western countries. Christmas, for example, is celebrated on January 7.

Russian Cyrillic letter	Sounds like . . .
Д	D as in **d**ress
Ж	Zh as in mea**s**ure
Ф	F as in **f**arm
Ш	Sh as in fi**sh**
Ю	Yu as in **U**se

CHAPTER 2
A Princess Arrives

During his long rule (1462–1505), Ivan the Great expanded Russia's territory and army. By his time, white limestone had replaced the Kremlin's log walls. Ivan went further: He ordered new brick walls to better withstand cannon fire.

Ivan also wanted to make the buildings in the Kremlin more like those found in the great cities of Europe. Some of Ivan's building plans didn't work out. One new cathedral collapsed before it was finished! So he began to look outside Russia for master builders. And after his first wife died, Ivan also turned to Europe for a new bride.

On June 24, 1472, a princess called Sofia set off from sunny Rome, Italy, for the far north. Her caravan included many people and a hundred

horses. On her five-
month journey, Sofia
visited grand cities
like Florence and
Bologna in Italy. She
crossed the Alps near
the Austrian city of
Innsbruck. She
passed through
Nuremberg,
a walled city in
Germany.

Princess Sofia,
wife of Ivan the Great

Sofia brought with her many books and rare
manuscripts in Latin, Greek, and Hebrew to
form the heart of a great library. But where is it
today? Were these priceless books lost in some
long-ago fire? Or is the lost library, even now,
hidden away in a forgotten Kremlin tunnel? No
one knows for sure.

Princess Sofia must have been disappointed

when she finally arrived at the fort. The shabby Kremlin buildings couldn't compare to the wonders she'd seen in Europe.

Soon after, Ivan sent for more Italian master builders. Although not much from this time survived, visitors can still wonder at the Palace of Facets. It gets its name from the sharp polished white stones that shine like the facets, or sides, of diamonds.

In 1475, Ivan hired Italian architect Aristotele Fioravanti to build a new Kremlin cathedral on the same spot as the first stone church. The new enormous Dormition Cathedral was made of limestone and took four years to finish. It is the oldest building in the Kremlin and the most important church in Russia. Inside, golden chandeliers light up priceless art. Topped by five golden domes, it's one of seven beautiful buildings in the Kremlin's Cathedral Square.

After finishing it in 1479, the architect wanted to return to Italy. But Ivan insisted he stay to build a bridge and train blacksmiths to make cannons. The story goes that Ivan even threatened to imprison Fioravanti if he refused. Ivan got his way: Fioravanti kept working in Russia until his death in 1486.

Dormition Cathedral, present day

The Frozen Market

The Moscow River, at the foot of the Kremlin, became a frozen market in winter. In the 1470s, one Italian visitor described a fantastic scene. "On this frozen river may be seen, daily, numbers of cows and pigs, great quantities of corn, wood, hay, and every other necessity. . . . Horses run on this river when it is frozen, and a good deal of amusement takes place."

One could get all sorts of things, the Italian reported, including a skinned cow, frozen whole, standing upright on four legs! Although Christmas markets still take place in Moscow, it might be hard to find an entire skinned cow.

Instead, crowds gather in Red Square to watch fireworks and hear the bells of the Kremlin Chimes, a massive twenty-five-ton clock on the Kremlin's famous Spasskaya Tower, ring in the New Year.

CHAPTER 3
Ivan the Terrible

Princess Sofia and Ivan III had eleven children. Their eldest son, Vasily, ruled after his father died. After Vasily III's death in 1533, Ivan IV came to power. He's best known as Ivan the Terrible.

Ivan was only three when he lost his father. Powerful men called regents took charge until

Ivan the Terrible

he was old enough to rule. They wanted total control. They starved Ivan's two uncles to death in a Kremlin dungeon. Ivan came to power on January 16, 1547, when he was sixteen. He was the first prince to call himself czar of all of Russia. *Czar* comes from the word *caesar*, a Roman title meaning "emperor."

Ivan, however, soon began playing this ruthless game of power himself. At age thirteen, he took part in a plot to murder a noble he felt was a threat. The man was thrown into the Kremlin kennels and killed by ferocious dogs.

Ivan's first marriage took place shortly afterward. But this happy time at court was followed by disaster. A mild, dry spring caused a terrible fire. Flames destroyed the Kremlin's Annunciation Cathedral. Nearly four thousand people in the city of Moscow died. Many more lost their houses.

Ivan hired artists and craftsmen to repair Kremlin buildings and paint new icons and murals. Today, visitors can see artwork created after the fire in the Annunciation Cathedral, which is topped by nine golden domes.

A few years later, in 1555, Ivan began to build St. Basil's Cathedral to celebrate his military victories that expanded Russian lands. This world-famous landmark stands in Red Square, just outside the Kremlin's walls. Eight of its colorful onion-shaped domes were built in honor of Ivan's battles. The ninth dome was named for Basil the Blessed, a Moscow holy man.

St. Basil's Cathedral

St. Basil's isn't the only church in Russia topped by colorful onion-shaped domes. The shape may have been borrowed from architecture in Muslim countries. It's also possible the domes were built to make the church appear taller or to help protect the roof from heavy snowfall. To some people, the onion domes look like burning candles.

Ivan the Terrible was often at war. As he fought to control his empire, Ivan became very suspicious of others. He thought other nobles were plotting against him. He didn't hesitate to have enemies executed. For instance, in 1570, Ivan feared a betrayal in the Russian city of Novgorod. He and his troops stormed the town and killed thousands.

In 1581, Ivan's violent temper had tragic results. His son's wife, Elena, was expecting a baby. One day, she didn't feel well, so she wasn't wearing all the layers of robes required for high-ranking women. This made Ivan so angry he hit her with his wooden staff, causing Elena to lose her baby.

Her husband, the prince, argued with his father about it. Ivan struck him with the staff, too. The prince died five days later. It's said that every night for months, the czar scratched the walls in agony. But Ivan couldn't change the awful thing he'd done.

CHAPTER 4
The Romanovs Come to Power

When Ivan the Terrible died in 1584, his son Fyodor became czar. Fyodor didn't care much about ruling. In fact, the country was mostly run by his brother-in-law, Boris Godunov. Fyodor died without an heir (someone to take his place). He was the last ruler in the line going back to Ivan I.

Boris Godunov

Boris Godunov took over. His death in April 1605 occurred during the Time of Troubles. It was a period of unrest. Russia faced famine because of poor harvests and invaders from Poland. Noble families fought for power and riches. Bandits roamed the streets of Moscow.

That's when a man called the False Dmitry appeared. He spun quite a tale. Another of Ivan the Terrible's sons named Dmitry was said to have died mysteriously as a boy. But the False Dmitry claimed to be him. He said that instead of being killed years before, he'd been smuggled to safety. Now he had returned to take his place on the throne.

Who was the False Dmitry? Could his story have been true? Most historians think the False Dmitry was a runaway monk pretending to be Ivan's dead son.

In any case, his rule lasted less than a year. One night, attackers from a rival family came

after him. Dmitry jumped out of a window and broke his leg. He was then shot to death. His body was displayed for all of Moscow to see. One man counted twenty-one wounds and said that Dmitry's skull had been crushed.

More years of turmoil followed. Finally, Mikhail Romanov was chosen as czar and crowned in 1613. Mikhail wasn't a strong leader. His father, the head of the Russian Orthodox Church, ruled alongside him. Still, with Mikhail Romanov a new dynasty began. The Romanov family stayed in power until the Russian Revolution in 1917— an incredible three hundred years.

During the Time of Troubles, many Kremlin buildings had been looted and damaged. Once again, it was time to repair and rebuild. And once again, Russia's leaders looked outside their borders to create palaces fit for an emperor.

Architects, builders, jewelers, and artists arrived from Persia, Germany, and Great Britain. The lovely Terem Palace, which still stands, was built in 1635–1636. It's topped by a gilded, painted roof visible from far away.

Petition Window

One feature of the Terem Palace is the Petition Window. (A petition is a written request for something.) From it, the czar would lower a box in which people could place their requests.

Did the ruler listen to his people? Probably not. We can guess that from a Russian expression that says if you put your problem "in a long box" nothing will happen very soon.

People in seventeenth-century Moscow battled fires and disease. In 1654, bubonic plague, also called the Black Death, struck Moscow. This disease often spread from rats to humans through flea bites. Thousands died. It's said that pigs and dogs roamed the streets eating corpses left behind.

The ruler at this time, Czar Aleksei, escaped the epidemic. But to make sure he wouldn't get sick in the future, he sent servants to find three unicorn horns. Of course, unicorns don't really exist. However, Vikings believed that the long tusks of a small whale called the narwhal were unicorn horns. These were thought to have magical healing powers. When people became more familiar with narwhals, the myth of real unicorns faded.

Narwhal

Toward the end of the 1600s, another Romanov emperor, Peter the Great, took charge. His rule would bring enormous changes to the Kremlin—and all of Russia.

CHAPTER 5
Peter the Great

Peter the Great came to power with a vision for Russia to become a more modern, powerful nation. In 1682, when he was only ten, he was named co-czar with his half-brother, Ivan V. However, since both were still boys, Ivan's older sister, Sophia, became regent.

Peter the Great

This turned out to be a good thing for Peter. He spent most of his time away from court at a royal lodge outside Moscow. There, the curious Peter could spend time learning about the rest of the world.

He was interested in seafaring. As a boy he loved to play soldiers and was fascinated by all things military. He grew to be well over six feet tall.

When Ivan V died in 1696, Peter ruled alone. In 1697, he set out on a tour of Europe. Peter learned best by doing: He traveled under an assumed name so he could work as a carpenter and learn to build ships.

Peter used what he learned to make Russia

more like advanced countries such as France and Great Britain. He developed a more modern army and navy. He took steps to separate the church from the government. He created a Senate of ten men to help run the country.

And Peter would end up building more than ships. After a bad Kremlin fire in 1701, Peter decided to create a new capital city for Russia. In 1703, he founded St. Petersburg, about four hundred miles northwest of Moscow. The city sits at the mouth of the Neva River, which spills into the Gulf of Finland on the Baltic Sea. Czars were still crowned in the Kremlin, but St. Petersburg became Russia's capital from 1712 until 1918.

Money for Peter's military and building projects had to come from somewhere. He squeezed more taxes out of the church and the gentry, or landowning class. In turn, landlords demanded more from the people who did the hard farmwork: Russia's peasants and serfs.

Serfs

Since medieval times, Russia's upper class had owned most of the land. By 1724, 97 percent of the Russians lived in rural areas. But few farmers owned the land they worked. Instead, they were peasants or serfs.

Serfs had even fewer rights than peasants. Serfs were basically slaves, the property of landlords who took most of their harvest.

Serfdom in Russia did not end until 1861.

St. Petersburg, 1703

CHAPTER 6
Catherine the Great

Peter wanted St. Petersburg to be Russia's "window on Europe." One of his successors, Catherine II, sometimes called Catherine the Great, felt the same. Catherine was a German princess who married her cousin, Peter III, in 1745. In 1762, she took part in a plot to overthrow her own husband. He was killed, and she became empress.

Catherine and her court lived in splendor in the Winter Palace in St. Petersburg. (Today, it's part of the Hermitage Museum.)

Catherine the Great

Catherine also shared Peter the Great's dreams for a powerful Russia and expanded its territory. She loved French culture and even made French the language of the court. However, Catherine didn't entirely forget about the Kremlin, which stood for Russia's past. Catherine once called it "this ancient and wonderful place."

Inside the Winter Palace in St. Petersburg

One later visitor agreed, saying that while St. Petersburg felt like an international city, "in Moscow, Russia enveloped us. . . . Moscow was Asiatic rather than European. . . . It had color and grandeur—spires which like minarets pierced the sky, and churches which, like their gilded domes, looked like mosques [Muslim places of worship]."

Catherine knew the Kremlin needed work. Although she'd worn a crown with five thousand diamonds at her coronation, one Kremlin church had trees growing through its roof. However, her plans to rebuild never amounted to much. But Catherine the Great took on other projects. She started new schools in towns. She opened Russia's first schools for girls of the nobility and the landowning class. She supported book publishing, science, and the arts.

In 1774, Catherine fell in love with a bold military leader named Grigory Potemkin. When Russia took over territory in the Crimea, near the Black Sea, she put him in charge.

Catherine and others toured the area in 1787. Potemkin wanted to impress his important visitors, so he decorated the villages. He put on shows with peasants singing. Today, the term "Potemkin village" means tricking someone into thinking a thing is better than it is.

But just as with Peter the Great, Catherine's projects and military efforts took money. Once more, the tax burden fell mostly on Russia's poor peasants and serfs. Under Catherine's reign, their lives got worse. New laws gave even more control to landlords and made it easier for masters to punish serfs. Serfs weren't allowed to go to the empress or government to protest or they would be punished. By 1794–1796, serfs made up nearly half of Russian's entire population of approximately twenty-nine million.

Catherine's son, Paul, took the throne after her death in 1796. Under Catherine, serfdom had spread. Paul did the same, giving land and serfs to his favorite noblemen. He also put down any peasant protests. Paul was very unpopular, with an awful temper. Like his mother, Paul planned to improve the run-down Kremlin. Before he could act, his enemies at court came into his bedroom one night in 1801 and beat him to death.

The next czar was Catherine's grandson Alexander I. This ruler also had enemies to worry about—thousands and thousands of them.

CHAPTER 7
The Great Fire of Moscow

The French general Napoleon Bonaparte was a powerful military leader. He expanded his empire in Europe. In 1812, he decided to invade Russia. In June, Napoleon's army of six hundred thousand men stormed into the country. Moscow was in their sights. A Russian military officer named Prince Mikhail Kutuzov rallied his troops to fight the invaders.

Prince Mikhail Kutuzov

An immense battle took place on September 7, 1812, in a village less than a hund miles from Moscow. Tens of thousands of men on both sides were killed. The corpses of thirty-five thousand horses were left on the field.

Commander Kutuzov came to realize that Moscow couldn't hold out. Muscovites (citizens of Moscow) fled for their lives. The Kremlin's cannons were cleaned and made ready to fire.

Some of the Kremlin's historic treasures were carted away or buried under the fort's thick walls. Besides priceless art, the Kremlin held precious necklaces and bracelets made by Russian goldsmiths. There were silver and gold platters, goblets, chalices, and ladles inlaid with pearls.

Ladle with pearls

When Napoleon arrived in Moscow, he found empty houses and deserted streets. Still, to one French general, the city seemed a wonderful prize: "A single sunbeam made this superb city glitter with a thousand varied colors."

But the Russians didn't intend to let the French invaders enjoy their city. Moscow's governor had something else in mind. On the night of September 14, as Napoleon's troops stood on the Kremlin's towers, they saw the dark skies begin to turn bright red. Fire!

The governor had left policemen behind in Moscow with orders to destroy major buildings. Other fires started. Flames spread rapidly in the town, where the old wooden buildings were crowded together and separated by narrow alleys. Soon all Moscow was in flames, though the Kremlin was mostly spared.

Napoleon Bonaparte (1769–1821)

Napoleon Bonaparte was a French general who became emperor. He was known for his military skills and efforts to expand the French empire.

Napoleon also started reforms in France. The most important was the Napoleonic Code, a system of codes and laws established in 1804. It provided written laws to be followed by everyone in society. It replaced old practices that favored the nobles. However, the code still gave men more rights than women.

After being defeated by the British at the Battle of Waterloo in June 1815, Napoleon was forced out of power. His son took over the throne. Napoleon was sent to live in exile on a remote island off the coast of Africa. He died there in 1821.

Napoleon and his officers barely escaped with their lives. One general said, "We were walking on a soil of fire, under a sky of fire, and between walls of fire." Moscow burned for six days, leaving only ashes and the smell of death.

Afterward, the French soldiers who remained took out their revenge on the Kremlin. They turned its churches into horse stables. They melted down nearly twelve thousand pounds of silver objects they found. It's said they even opened the coffins of ancient saints to look for gold.

The final act of revenge came in October, when Napoleon ordered barrels of explosives laid around several Kremlin buildings and towers. Then they were set off. When he heard the explosion, Napoleon declared, "The Kremlin ancient citadel . . . this palace of the Czars, has ceased to exist."

Napoleon was wrong. The Kremlin wasn't totally destroyed. And on the battlefields, Russian soldiers held out. They all waited for the harsh winter to come. They knew the French would suffer from the cold and lack

of supplies. Sure enough, French troops were forced to retreat by the end of the year.

Once again, Moscow and the Kremlin had survived.

After the Great Fire of Moscow, the Kremlin was repaired. Moats were filled in to become new gardens. The golden domes of the cathedrals gleamed in the sunshine once more. People could look up to this shining place on the hill with pride.

Outside the Kremlin's walls, Moscow was in much worse shape. More than half of Moscow's nine thousand buildings were in ruins. But the Great Fire of Moscow also brought a chance to make the old city more modern.

New fountains, oil street lights, and sewer drains were added. Streets were widened. To prevent future fires, a new fire department with more than 1,000 men and 450 horses was established.

Rebuilding took years. But it was worth it. As one citizen wrote, "Moscow is becoming beautiful."

The Kremlin, 1813

Ivan the Great Bell Tower

When Napoleon occupied the Kremlin, he wanted the gold from the cross on the top of the famous Ivan the Great Bell Tower, the tallest structure in the fort. It turned out to be not gold but only gilded wood.

And though he ordered the bell tower to be destroyed, it survived. Today, its largest bell weighs seventy tons. Tourists can climb this impressive building to gaze out over all of Moscow.

CHAPTER 8
The Russian Revolution

Czar Nicholas II was born in 1868. His coronation took place in the Kremlin in 1896. That would never happen again. Nicholas was not only the final Romanov ruler; he was Russia's last czar.

Czar Nicholas II's coronation, 1896

Czar Nicholas II and his family

Nicholas and his empress, Alexandra, a granddaughter of England's Queen Victoria, had four daughters and one son. They were the richest royal family in the world. They lived in the Winter Palace in St. Petersburg. They were fabulously wealthy, owning jewels, gold, and land worth billions. One American visitor who attended a palace ball in 1902 described stairs "adorned by a magnificent display of gold plate fixed to the walls." There were hundreds of footmen wearing scarlet red. The ballroom shimmered in the light of chandeliers.

The Romanovs loved to collect precious objects, especially fantastic jeweled Easter eggs made by Peter Carl Fabergé, a Russian master goldsmith. Czar Nicholas II ordered an egg for his mother and for his wife each Easter.

Coronation egg

A total of fifty imperial eggs were made between 1885 and 1916. The first egg Nicholas gave Alexandra was called the Rosebud. The diamond-crusted egg opens to reveal a beautiful flower inside. Another, the Coronation egg, contains a miniature gold-and-red carriage. Today, some of the imperial eggs are in the Kremlin Armory Chamber. Others are scattered in collections around the world. Seven are lost.

Like emperors of the past, Czar Nicholas and his family lived in luxury. (Although Alexandra, who was shy, and had grown up in Germany, had simpler tastes than most Russian nobles.) Their one-hundred-room Alexander Palace was surrounded by a tall fence and guards. The gardens contained paths, a lake, and even an elephant. Inside, they could enjoy a saltwater pool, two grand pianos, and hundreds of paintings mounted on walls with silk wallpaper.

But at the same time, most people in Russia

The Billiard Hall in Alexander Palace

were still poor—and getting angrier than ever about their lives. Serfdom had been officially ended by Nicholas's grandfather, Czar Alexander II, in 1861 (the same year America's Civil War over slavery began). But there was still unrest.

Treasures of the Armory

Ten imperial eggs are on display in the Kremlin's famous Armory Chamber, which became a museum in 1851. The Armory's nine halls house more than four thousand treasures from Russia's past, including paintings, royal robes, silverware, and ornate carriages.

Visitors can admire golden crowns, gorgeous thrones, and jeweled scepters. There are cases filled with silver and gold plates, cups, pitchers, and bowls encrusted with sparkling precious stones.

The Armory's collection of weaponry dates back to the twelfth century. It includes rare shields, swords, and sabers decorated with silver, gold, and other jewels. You can step into the past and imagine yourself competing at a joust or donning a suit of mail to stand guard high on the Kremlin walls.

In 1881, a bomb killed Alexander II. He was assassinated by a member of a group that wanted to change the government and get rid of all czars. People protested food shortages and unfair working conditions. A wave of change swept the nation. This time it could not be stopped.

The assassination of Czar Alexander II, 1881

On January 22, 1905, a peaceful Sunday protest turned into a tragedy. Police killed more than one hundred people outside the Winter Palace in St. Petersburg. Even though Czar Nicholas wasn't there, the Bloody Sunday event fueled a revolt. The massacre helped set in motion a civil war called the Russian Revolution. The revolution led to a complete change in how Russia was governed.

Bloody Sunday, 1905

In March 1917, Nicholas II bowed to pressure and left the throne. The long line of Romanov rule ended. Nicholas, Alexandra, and their five children were placed under house arrest.

A temporary government was put in place. Soon a group called the Bolsheviks took over. *Bolshevik* is a word meaning "bigger," "more," or "majority." The Bolshevik army of peasants and workers was called the Red Army. The leader's name was Vladimir Lenin.

Vladimir Lenin

Communism

By 1925, the Bolshevik Party had been renamed the Communist Party, which is still in power in Russia today. *Communism* is a system of government in which property, such as mines, factories, and businesses, is owned by the government instead of by private individuals. This is the opposite of *capitalism*, the system used in the United States, where people are free to work for themselves to start a business or market an idea or product. Communists follow the teachings of Karl Marx (1818–1883) and his 1848 book, *The Communist Manifesto*.

Karl Marx

The Romanov family hoped to be allowed to leave Russia. It was not to be. In the early morning hours of July 17, 1918, on Lenin's orders, Nicholas and Alexandra, along with their son and four daughters, were all shot to death. Their bodies were taken to the forest and buried in shallow graves.

The murder of the imperial family showed just how much the new Russia had split with the past. Communist leaders made many promises about the future. Lenin pledged there would be no difference between rich and poor. Instead of a few people having riches while others starved, everyone would have enough to live decently. Desperately poor citizens wanted to believe him.

Anastasia

Anastasia was the czar's youngest daughter. Just a few years after the Romanovs were murdered, rumors began to spread that Anastasia had escaped and survived. Several impostors pretended to be her. The world became fascinated by Anastasia.

In 1976, the bones of the emperor and empress and three of their daughters were found in the forest. The discovery was kept secret for a long time.

But what about Alexei, the only son? And Anastasia? Finally, in 2007, an amateur historian exploring the forest discovered the bones of a Romanov boy—Alexei—and a girl, not far from where the other Romanovs had been buried. There could no longer be any doubt: Scientists now had identified the remains of four daughters and one son. Anastasia had died with her family.

Lenin didn't want to stay in St. Petersburg, which had been renamed Petrograd. It had been the home of Russia's imperial families for too long. So in March 1918, Lenin moved the capital back to the Kremlin in Moscow.

Would the new government care about the Kremlin's treasures from Russia's past? In fact, in 1922, many priceless religious paintings and objects were sold off. But, once again, the Kremlin managed to survive.

The country did more than change its capital. It changed its name. In 1922, Russia became the Soviet Union, or the USSR (Union of Soviet Socialist Republics). The USSR began by dividing imperial Russia into four separate areas, or republics. Each republic fell under the control of the Kremlin. By 1990, the USSR had taken over twenty different republics, such as Armenia and Lithuania, as well as many other provinces and regions.

USSR flag

After Lenin died in 1924, Joseph Stalin (1878–1953) came to power. By 1928, Stalin had become dictator, a ruler with total personal control. No one was safe—not generals, officials, artists, or teachers. Ordinary citizens lived in fear of being purged—sent to a harsh labor camp or killed. Historians believe that between two and three million were killed during Stalin's rule. Stalin's policies, especially his failed "five-year plans" to improve the economy, caused additional deaths as well. Five million people died in the famine of 1930–1933.

During the "Great Purge" of the 1930s, Stalin went after anyone he imagined opposed him. People were terrified of being falsely accused—and many were. Children were encouraged to turn in anyone who spoke against the government—even their parents. No wonder people feared to work or live in the Kremlin, known as Stalin's "Red Fortress."

Joseph Stalin

The Kremlin Fox

Nikolai Bukharin, a Bolshevik leader, was one of Stalin's many victims. He was falsely accused of being a spy and killed in 1938. Bukharin loved animals and kept many pets, including a hawk, snakes, hedgehogs, and a fox.

Long after his death, Bukharin's fox could be spotted in the Kremlin, playing hide-and-seek in the gardens. Unlike many others during those dark days, the fox was able to remain free.

CHAPTER 9
World War II

By 1939, Adolf Hitler and the Nazi Party had taken power in Germany. On August 23 of that year, the Soviet Union and Germany signed the Hitler-Stalin Pact, sometimes called the Nazi-Soviet Pact. The two countries agreed not to become enemies or attack each other.

Adolf Hitler

On September 1, Germany invaded Poland. That caused Great Britain and France to declare war on Germany. World War II began on September 3, 1939.

Because of the Hitler-Stalin Pact, the USSR didn't enter the war. But Hitler didn't keep his promises to Stalin. On June 22, 1941, Hitler launched a surprise attack on the Soviet Union. More than three million soldiers, three thousand tanks, and 2,500 aircraft invaded the country.

Fighting was fierce. By late fall, Hitler's troops were within twenty miles of Moscow. The enemy circled the city on three sides. Just as in 1812, the Kremlin was in danger. Treasures were spirited away for safekeeping. Golden domes were draped in black to hide them from enemy bombers. Fake buildings were erected to confuse attackers from the air.

Stalin made the Kremlin his headquarters. He liked to have pictures taken that showed him at work. He wanted his people to see him as totally in charge.

Germany almost took over the Soviet Union. But just like in 1812, the harsh northern winters helped save the day. German troops weren't prepared for the bitter cold and lack of food in the winter of 1941–1942. They fell back, although they didn't give up all the land they'd won.

Germany tried again, launching attacks in the summer of 1942 and again in 1943. But the Red Army held on and slowly began pushing the invaders out.

The Soviet Union had switched sides the day it was invaded. It joined the Allied nations, including Great Britain, France, and in late 1941, the United States. During the war, Stalin worked with British prime minister Winston Churchill and US president Franklin D. Roosevelt to plan Allied strategy.

Joseph Stalin, Franklin D. Roosevelt, and Winston Churchill, 1943

The Allied invasion of Normandy, France, on June 6, 1944, opened a second battlefront in Europe, putting more pressure on Hitler's forces. The Soviets joined the United States and Great Britain in driving the Germans back to Berlin. Hitler committed suicide on April 30, 1945, and Germany surrendered on May 7. World War II ended when Japan surrendered on September 2,

1945, after atomic bombs were dropped on Hiroshima and Nagasaki.

At the Kremlin, victory against Germany was celebrated on June 24, 1945. Grateful citizens stood in the pouring rain to thank and honor the soldiers.

But another, very different kind of war was about to begin.

The Invasion of Normandy

The Nuclear Age

In 1941, the United States began working on developing an atomic bomb. Toward the end of World War II, the United States decided to use a bomb to force Japan to surrender.

An atomic bomb has great explosive power because it splits the atoms of heavy elements such as plutonium and uranium. Elements like plutonium are radioactive and have harmful biological effects on humans.

On August 6, 1945, the nuclear age began when the United States dropped an atomic bomb on the Japanese city of Hiroshima, killing seventy thousand men, women, and children. (The death toll had risen to one hundred thousand by year's end.) On August 9, a second bomb dropped on Nagasaki killed about forty thousand. Japan quickly surrendered, ending the war.

Atomic bomb blast over Nagasaki, Japan

CHAPTER 10
The Cold War

The Soviet Union had sided with the Allies since the day Germany invaded in June 1941. But the end of the war brought new tensions between the USSR and Western democracies. The United States worried the Soviet Union would take over other countries, many in Southeast Asia and Africa. The United States wanted to keep that from happening.

Soviet soldiers in Berlin at the end of World War II, 1945

The term Cold War is used to describe these tensions and this period. It lasted from about 1947 until 1991. There were no actual battles, but the threat of war was constant.

KGB emblem

The two superpowers, the United States and the USSR, spied on one another to get information. In the Soviet Union, a spy organization called the KGB (in English, the Committee for State Security) was begun in 1954. It was a bit like America's CIA (Central Intelligence Agency). The KGB spied on other countries and its own citizens, too.

During the Cold War, the United States and the Soviet Union were engaged in a nuclear arms race. In other words, each nation tried to increase its weapons to scare the other. One fear was that one of the countries would drop another atomic bomb like the ones that had ended World War II in Japan.

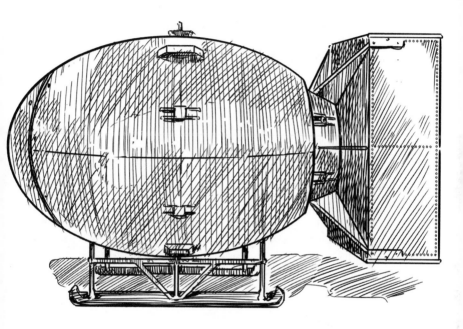

A nuclear device similar to the
one dropped over Nagasaki

Today, the world continues to face the challenge of controlling nuclear weapons and making sure nuclear power plants operate safely.

Chernobyl

The worst nuclear power plant accident in history occurred in Russia at Chernobyl in 1986, about five hundred miles from Moscow. The

explosion caused the leak of radioactive materials to the surrounding area. The Soviet government tried but could not cover up the accident because radioactivity was detected in the wind.

It's thought that about fifty people died and many more later became sick from the effects of radiation. About 1,600 square miles around Chernobyl are still blocked off as unsafe for human habitation.

When Joseph Stalin died in March 1953, Nikita Khrushchev took over. In 1956, Khrushchev condemned some of Stalin's worst crimes. This led to an effort to rule with less violence and terror. Under Stalin, the Kremlin hadn't been open to the public. Now visitors were welcomed again.

Nikita Khrushchev

But the USSR remained a repressive nation. There were no free elections. It was hard for people to express their own ideas. Most ordinary people struggled just to get enough to eat. And while the Kremlin invested in military equipment, plans for improving industry, agriculture, housing, and access to food for ordinary citizens fell short. People often had to wait in long lines, trying to buy beef, mutton, carrots, and cabbage. One man in 1982 told a visitor, "You're lucky to find butter at all."

Nikita Khrushchev was forced out in 1964 by a group led by Leonid Brezhnev. Brezhnev died in 1982. In 1985, Mikhail Gorbachev took over. Gorbachev began a policy called *glasnost* (openness), which permitted more open discussion of politics, criticism of government, and a freer press. This openness led to dramatic changes in the Soviet Union. The Communist Party had less power, and elections became fairer.

Meeting between US president Ronald Reagan
and Mikhail Gorbachev, 1986

In the end, the policy of glasnost led to Gorbachev's end. As more people spoke up, opposition grew in the countries under Soviet control. Beginning in the spring of 1989, a wave of revolutions took place in Eastern Europe. Communist governments crumpled in Poland, Hungary, Romania, and Czechoslovakia.

President Gorbachev resigns, 1991

On December 25, 1991, Gorbachev spoke on television to announce his resignation as president. The Soviet Union had collapsed. Boris Yeltsin had been president of Russia when it was part of the USSR. Yeltsin became president of the new Russia, the Russian Federation.

Boris Yeltsin

The Russian flag once more flew over the Kremlin. On New Year's in 1992, the chimes of the Kremlin bells could barely be heard over Moscow's fireworks.

The new Russia was supposed to become a democracy. But would that really happen?

CHAPTER 11
Russia in the Twenty-First Century

In 2000, Vladimir Putin became president of Russia. Putin was born in 1952 in St. Petersburg, Russia. After studying law, he became an intelligence officer—basically a spy—for the KGB. He began his career in government in 1991 and rose quickly. When the Soviet Union dissolved, the KGB was broken into several agencies. In 1998, Putin was made director of one called the Federal Security Services (FSS), which handles internal security and counterintelligence.

Russian president
Vladimir Putin

Russian soldiers invade Crimea, 2014

Under Putin, Russia has an authoritarian government. This means the leader or a small group at the top is in control and can operate without following laws or a constitution. Often, newspapers, television, and other media outlets are under this group's control. People with opposing views are prevented from speaking out, writing newspaper articles, or running for office. Elections aren't free or fair.

Western democracies condemn Putin's policies. In 2014, Putin invaded Crimea, an independent region in the country of Ukraine. Russia has used the Internet and spies to try to affect how people vote in other countries, including in the 2016 US presidential election. Russian journalists and opposition leaders have died in mysterious circumstances. In 2018, Russia used a deadly nerve gas to poison a former spy in Great Britain.

Putin won a March 2018 election for a fourth six-year term, but the election was rigged. No one

Vladimir Putin at a presidential rally near the Kremlin, 2018

knows how long Putin will remain in power.

Is there any hope for real democracy in Russia someday? The way things are now, the answer would be no.

Much has changed in the seven hundred years since Ivan I and Peter first laid the stone of their new cathedral on the top of a riverside hill. Today, the Kremlin, along with Red Square, is a UNESCO World Heritage site. That means the United Nations believes it's an important place of culture and history that should be protected for future generations.

Within its walls, visitors are reminded of the power of art. They are awed by the Kremlin's beauty and treasures. It's harder to make out what lies behind the glitter—tales of secrets, spies, betrayal, and murder.

But one thing is almost certain: the Kremlin will survive.

Can You Find a Missing Treasure?

Russia is famous for its incredible jeweled Easter eggs. Of the original fifty, there used to be eight missing imperial Fabergé eggs. Then, in 2014, a scrap gold dealer in the United States bought an ornament for $14,000. While searching the internet, he realized what he actually had was a Fabergé egg.

The egg was sold to a private collector. Although the sale price wasn't revealed, a similar egg was sold in 2007 for nearly $20 million. That leaves seven eggs still missing.

Maybe you'll find one—or some other Kremlin treasure—someday.

Timeline of the Kremlin

1156 — First record of wooden fort on Kremlin site

1237 — Mongols invade Russia and destroy Kremlin wooden buildings by fire

1325 — Ivan I begins a sixteen-year rule of Moscow

1326 — Ivan I lays the foundation stone for the Kremlin's Dormition Cathedral

1367 — Following a fire, Dmitry Donskoi replaces wooden walls with white limestone

1475 — Ivan III hires Italian architect Aristotele Fioravanti to build a new Dormition Cathedral

1547 — Ivan the Terrible comes to power at age sixteen

1703 — Peter the Great builds St. Petersburg, the new capital of Russia

1812 — The Great Fire of Moscow during the invasion by Napoleon

1838 — Construction of the Grand Kremlin Palace launched

1917 — Following the Russian Revolution, the capital moves back to the Kremlin

1924 — Vladimir Lenin dies and is soon succeeded by Joseph Stalin

1941 — Kremlin buildings are disguised to avoid German bombers

1990 — Kremlin is designated a World Heritage site

1991 — The Soviet Union collapses

1999 — Boris Yeltsin resigns and Vladimir Putin becomes president

2018 — Vladimir Putin wins a fourth term as president

Timeline of the World

1206	Genghis Khan unifies Mongolia and begins to expand his empire
1789	George Washington inaugurated as first president of the United States
1861	Civil War begins in the United States of America
1912	The *Titanic* sinks
1914	World War I begins
1920	The Nineteenth Amendment is ratified, giving US women voting rights
1929	The Great Depression begins in the United States
1939	World War II begins
1945	United States drops two atomic bombs on Japan, ending World War II
1963	Martin Luther King Jr. gives "I Have a Dream" speech
1969	Human beings land on the moon
1989	The Berlin Wall begins to fall, signaling end to the Cold War
1994	Nelson Mandela elected president of South Africa
2008	Barack Obama elected first African American president of the United States
2014	Winter Olympics held in Sochi, Russia
2015	Elizabeth II becomes Great Britain's longest-reigning monarch

Bibliography

*Books for young readers

Ascher, Abraham. *The Kremlin.* New York: Newsweek, 1978.

Charles Rivers Editors. *The Moscow Kremlin: The History of Russia's Most Famous Landmark.* Wauwatosa, WI: Charles Rivers Editors, 2017.

*Fleming, Candace. *The Family Romanov: Murder, Rebellion, and the Fall of Imperial Russia.* New York: Schwartz & Wade, 2014.

Kelly, Laurence. *Moscow: A Traveller's Companion.* Northampton, MA: Interlink, 2005.

Merridale, Catherine. *Red Fortress: History and Illusion in the Kremlin.* New York: Metropolitan Books, Henry Holt and Company, 2013.

Riasanovsky, Nicholas V., and Mark D. Steinberg. *A History of Russia.* New York: Oxford University Press, 2011.

Sizov, E. S., *Treasures from the Kremlin: An Exhibition from the State Museums of the Moscow Kremlin.* New York, The Metropolitan Museum of Art. Exhibition catalog.

Vladimirskaya, Nonna, and Rimma Kostikova. *Art and History of the Kremlin of Moscow.* Moscow: Welcome Books, 1996.

Voyce, Arthur. *The Moscow Kremlin: Its History, Architecture, and Art Treasures.* Berkeley: University of California Press, 1954.

Websites

BBC Timeline of Russian History

http://www.bbc.com/news/world-europe-17840446

Britannica: Russia

https://www.britannica.com/place/Russia

Kremlin and Red Square: UNESCO World Heritage Site

http://whc.unesco.org/en/list/545

Moscow Kremlin Museums

http://www.kreml.ru/en-Us/museums-moscow-kremlin/

Visitor's Guide to Moscow

http://www.moscow.info/

WHoHQ

YOUR HEADQUARTERS *FOR* HISTORY

Activities, Mad Libs, and sidesplitting jokes!
Discover the Who HQ books beyond the biographies

ST. NICHOLAS TOWER

RED SQUARE

PRESIDENT'S RESIDENCE

IVAN THE GREAT BELL TOWER

ST. BASIL'S CATHEDRAL

ANNUNCIATION CATHEDRAL

PETER TOWER

The Kremlin's towers and redbrick walls

Spasskaya Tower

Cathedral Square, in the Kre

mlin

St. Basil's Cathedral

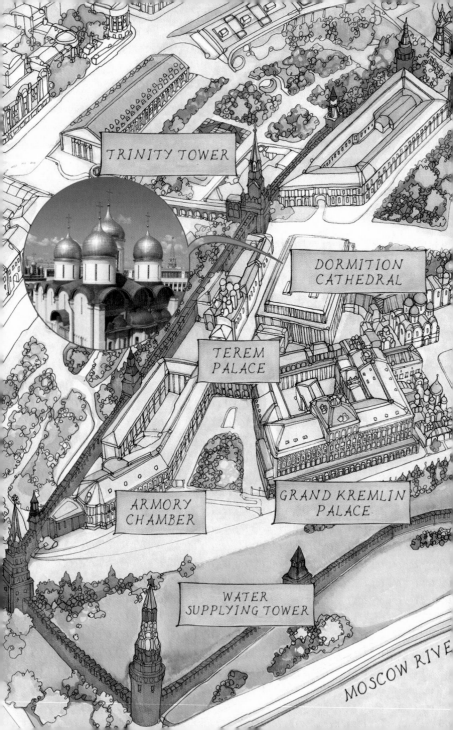

TRINITY TOWER

DORMITION
CATHEDRAL

TEREM
PALACE

ARMORY
CHAMBER

GRAND KREMLIN
PALACE

WATER
SUPPLYING TOWER

MOSCOW RIVE